EMPOWER HER:

A WOMAN ENTREPRENEUR'S GUIDE TO ACHIEVING DREAMS

9 781257 579693

Table of Contents

Chapter 1: Understanding the Power of Goals

The Importance of Goal Setting

Goal setting is a powerful tool that can transform your entrepreneurial journey. For women entrepreneurs, having a clear vision of what you want to achieve provides a roadmap to success. By defining specific, measurable, achievable, relevant, and time-bound (SMART) goals, you create a structured path that guides your daily actions. This clarity not only helps in focusing your efforts but also boosts your confidence as you see progress toward your aspirations.

In the competitive landscape of entrepreneurship and real estate, goal setting becomes even more critical. It allows you to identify opportunities and challenges ahead, making it easier to strategize effectively.

Customizable goal setting planners can be particularly beneficial, enabling you to tailor your goals to align with your personal and professional ambitions. These planners serve as a constant reminder of what you are working towards and help maintain your motivation.

Moreover, goal setting encourages accountability. Sharing your goals with peers or mentors creates a support system that holds you accountable for your progress. This is especially important for freelancers and solopreneurs who may lack the structured environment of a traditional workplace. When you articulate your goals, you invite others to check in on your progress, fostering a sense of community and collaboration that can drive you forward.

The emotional aspect of goal setting

cannot be overlooked. Setting goals gives you a sense of purpose and direction, which is essential for maintaining passion and motivation. As you achieve smaller milestones, the sense of accomplishment fuels your desire to reach even greater heights. For women in business, this emotional connection to your goals can be a significant factor in overcoming obstacles and staying resilient in the face of challenges.

Finally, revisiting and adjusting your goals regularly is crucial for sustained growth. As you progress, your priorities may shift, and new opportunities may arise. A guided goal setting planner can help you reflect on your achievements and recalibrate your goals accordingly. This flexibility ensures that your aspirations remain aligned with your evolving vision, propelling you toward success in your entrepreneurial endeavors.

The Psychology Behind Achieving Dreams

Achieving dreams is not just about setting goals; it involves understanding the psychology that drives our ambitions. The mind plays a crucial role in how we perceive our potential and the obstacles in our path. By tapping into our intrinsic motivation, we can align our goals with our values and passions, making the journey toward our dreams more fulfilling. This alignment acts as a compass, guiding you through the complexities of your ventures and helping you stay focused on what truly matters.

Self-belief is a powerful catalyst in the psychology of achieving dreams. Women often grapple with self-doubt, which can hinder their progress. By cultivating a positive mindset and practicing self-affirmation, entrepreneurs can build resilience and confidence. This shift in perception allows them to view challenges as opportunities for growth rather than insurmountable barriers. As they reinforce their belief in their capabilities, they become more likely to take the necessary risks to pursue their aspirations wholeheartedly.

Visualization techniques serve as another effective tool in the psychological arsenal for achieving dreams. By picturing themselves reaching their goals, entrepreneurs can create a mental roadmap that clarifies their objectives. This practice not only enhances focus but also strengthens emotional commitment to the desired outcome. Women entrepreneurs, in particular, can benefit from visualizing their success, as it fosters a sense of empowerment and helps eliminate self-imposed limitations that may have previously held them back.

Moreover, support networks play a vital role in the entrepreneurial journey. Surrounding oneself with like minded individuals can provide encouragement and inspiration. Engaging with mentors and peers who understand the unique challenges faced by women in business can offer invaluable insights and strategies. These relationships create a sense of community, reinforcing the belief that dreams are achievable and that one does not have to navigate the path alone.

Lastly, embracing a growth mindset is essential for sustaining progress toward dreams. This perspective encourages entrepreneurs to view failures as learning experiences rather than setbacks. By understanding that each challenge contributes to their development, women entrepreneurs can maintain their motivation and adapt their strategies as needed. In this way, the psychology behind achieving dreams becomes a continuous cycle of growth, resilience, and empowerment, ultimately leading to success in their ventures.

Overcoming Common

Goal Setting Barriers

Setting goals is essential for any entrepreneur, yet many face barriers that prevent them from achieving their dreams. One common challenge is the fear of failure. This fear can paralyze decision making and lead to procrastination. To overcome this, entrepreneurs should reframe their mindset, viewing failures as learning opportunities rather than setbacks. Embracing a growth mindset can empower women entrepreneurs to take bold steps towards their goals, knowing that each setback is a stepping stone to success.

Another significant barrier is lack of clarity regarding what one truly wants to achieve. Without clear goals, it's easy to become overwhelmed and lose focus. Women entrepreneurs can enhance their goal setting process by utilizing guided planners that encourage self-reflection and detailed planning. By breaking down larger goals into manageable tasks, they can create a structured pathway that fosters motivation and accountability.

Time management is also a critical aspect that can hinder goal achievement. Many entrepreneurs juggle multiple responsibilities, making it difficult to allocate time for goal oriented tasks. To combat this, women can adopt customizable planners that accommodate their unique schedules. By prioritizing tasks and setting aside specific time blocks for goal related activities, they can ensure consistent progress towards their aspirations.

Support systems play a vital role in overcoming barriers to goal setting. Surrounding oneself with like minded individuals can provide encouragement and inspiration. Women entrepreneurs should seek out mentorship, networking groups, or accountability partners who understand their journey. This sense of community not only fosters motivation but also creates opportunities for collaboration and growth.

Lastly, the fear of judgment can inhibit women from fully pursuing their goals. Entrepreneurs often worry about how others perceive their ambitions. To overcome this barrier, it's crucial to cultivate self-compassion and focus on personal growth rather than external validation. By embracing their unique journey and celebrating small victories, women can build confidence and resilience, propelling them closer to their ultimate goals.

Chapter 2: Crafting Your Vision

Defining Your Unique Entrepreneurial Journey

Every entrepreneur's journey is unique, shaped by their individual experiences, visions, and aspirations. Defining your entrepreneurial path starts with understanding what drives you. Reflect on your motivations—are they rooted in passion, the desire for independence, or the ambition to create change? This self-awareness will serve as a foundation for setting meaningful goals that resonate with your true self.

As you embark on this journey, it's essential to embrace your distinct qualities and strengths. These attributes not only differentiate you from others but also enhance your ability to overcome challenges. Whether you are a creative entrepreneur crafting innovative solutions or a real estate investor navigating market trends, acknowledging your unique skills will empower you to leverage them effectively in your goal setting process.

Developing a clear vision of what success looks like for you is crucial. Consider the legacy you wish to leave behind and the impact you want to make. Visualize your goals not just as achievements but as stepping stones toward fulfilling your larger purpose. This vision will guide you in creating a roadmap that aligns with your aspirations and motivates you to persevere through obstacles.

It's important to recognize that your entrepreneurial journey will include both triumphs and setbacks. Embrace the lessons that come from failures as they are just as valuable as your successes. Each experience provides insights that will refine your goals and strategies, helping you to adapt and grow. Celebrate your progress, no matter how small, as it contributes to your overall journey.

Finally, surround yourself with a supportive community that understands your journey. Networking with fellow entrepreneurs can offer encouragement and inspiration, as well as valuable resources. Sharing your experiences and learning from others will enrich your path and reinforce your commitment to achieving your dreams. Remember, your journey is not just about reaching the destination but also about enjoying the ride and the growth that comes with it.

Visualizing Your Success

Visualizing your success is an essential practice for any entrepreneur, especially for women navigating the challenges of the business world. When you create a vivid mental picture of your goals, you establish a powerful connection to the outcomes you desire. This visualization process not only boosts your motivation but also helps you to align your daily actions with your long-term aspirations. By focusing on the end result, you begin to see the path to success more clearly.

Incorporating visualization techniques into your goal setting planner can amplify your potential. Take time each day to imagine what success looks like for you. Picture your ideal work environment, the clients you serve, and the impact you have on your community. This practice encourages a positive mindset, allowing you to overcome obstacles and stay resilient in the face of challenges. The clearer your vision, the stronger your resolve to achieve it.

To further enhance your visualization practice, consider creating a vision board. A vision board is a collage of images, quotes, and symbols that represent your goals and dreams. This tangible representation serves as a daily reminder of what you are working

towards. As you engage with your vision board, it reinforces your commitment to your
goals, making the process of achievement feel more attainable and real.

It's also crucial to visualize not just the destination but the journey as well. Envision the steps you need to take, the skills you must develop, and the relationships you need to nurture. This holistic approach to visualization prepares you for the ups and downs that come with entrepreneurship. By anticipating challenges and picturing your responses, you can approach your journey with greater confidence and resilience.

Finally, remember that visualization is a dynamic practice. As you grow and evolve in your entrepreneurial journey, so too should your visions. Regularly revisit and update your visualizations to ensure they align with your current ambitions and aspirations. By continually refining your vision, you empower yourself to adapt and thrive in an ever changing business landscape, ultimately leading you closer to the success you envision.

Aligning Your Goals with

Your Values

Aligning your goals with your values is a crucial step in the journey of any entrepreneur, especially for women who often juggle multiple roles. When your goals reflect your core values, you not only gain clarity but also a strong sense of purpose that propels you forward. It's essential to take the time to identify what truly matters to you, as these values will serve as a compass in your decision making process, guiding you toward a fulfilling entrepreneurial path.

To begin this alignment, conduct a personal inventory of your values. Consider what drives you, what you stand for, and what you want to achieve in your business and life. This reflective practice can help you gain insights into your priorities, whether they be financial success, work-life balance, or community impact. By understanding your values, you can set goals that resonate deeply and inspire you to take action daily.

Next, evaluate your current goals in light of your identified values. Are they in harmony, or do you feel a disconnect? It's common for entrepreneurs to set goals based on external expectations or societal norms rather than their own values. Reassess your goals and make necessary adjustments to ensure they align with what you truly want. This alignment not only enhances motivation but also fosters resilience during challenging times.

Incorporating your values into your goal setting process can also enhance creativity and innovation. When you prioritize what matters most to you, your ideas flow more freely, and you become more open to exploring new opportunities. This is particularly relevant for creative entrepreneurs and freelancers who thrive on inspiration. By anchoring your goals in your values, you cultivate an environment where creativity can flourish, leading to greater satisfaction and success.

Finally, regularly revisit and reflect on your goals and values. As you evolve personally and professionally, your values may shift, and it's important to adapt your goals accordingly. Create a habit of checking in with yourself, ensuring that your aspirations continue to reflect your core beliefs. This ongoing process of alignment will not only empower you as a business owner but will also inspire others in your community to pursue their goals with intention and authenticity.

Chapter 3: Setting SMART Goals

What Are SMART Goals?

SMART goals are a powerful framework that can help entrepreneurs and real estate investors turn their dreams into actionable plans. The acronym SMART stands for Specific, Measurable, Achievable, Relevant, and Time-bound. By clearly defining goals within these parameters, entrepreneurs can create a roadmap that not only outlines their aspirations but also details the steps needed to achieve them.

Specificity is crucial in goal setting. Rather than saying, "I want to grow my business," a SMART goal would specify how much growth is desired and the methods to achieve it. For example, an entrepreneur might aim to increase sales by 20% over the next quarter through targeted marketing campaigns. This level of detail helps to eliminate ambiguity, allowing for a clearer focus on what needs to be accomplished.

Measurable goals enable entrepreneurs to track their progress. By incorporating quantifiable metrics, such as revenue targets or the number of new clients, individuals can regularly assess their advancement towards their goals. This measurement not only motivates but also provides valuable insights into what strategies are working and which may require adjustment.

Achievability is another vital aspect of SMART goals. While it's important to aim high, setting overly ambitious goals can lead to frustration and burnout. Entrepreneurs should evaluate their resources, skills, and time commitments to ensure that their goals are attainable. This realistic approach encourages persistence and fosters a sense of accomplishment when milestones are reached.

Lastly, ensuring that goals are relevant and time-bound ties everything together. Goals should align with one's broader business vision and have a clear deadline. By setting a timeline, such as completing a project by the end of the month, entrepreneurs can create urgency and maintain focus. In conclusion, adopting the SMART framework can empower women entrepreneurs to set goals that are not only inspiring but also practical and achievable, ultimately leading to their success.

Applying SMART Goals to Your Business

Setting goals is crucial for any entrepreneur, and using the SMART framework can significantly enhance your approach to achieving success. SMART stands for Specific, Measurable, Achievable, Relevant, and Time-bound. By applying this structured method, you can create clear objectives that guide your business decisions and strategies. It helps to break down your larger aspirations into actionable steps, making the journey toward your ambitions feel more manageable and less overwhelming.

Specificity is key when defining your goals. Instead of saying, "I want to increase sales," a SMART goal would be, "I want to increase my sales by 20% in the next quarter by launching a new marketing campaign." This clear definition not only sets a precise target but also helps you focus your efforts on what truly matters for your business. When your goals are specific, you can allocate resources more effectively to achieve them.

Measurable goals allow you to track your progress and celebrate small wins along the way. This aspect of the SMART framework ensures that you can quantify your success. For instance, if your goal is to grow your social media following, specify a number like "I will gain 500 new followers on Instagram by the end of the month." This measurement not only keeps you accountable but also motivates you to push through challenges as you see tangible results.

Achievability is about setting realistic goals that push you but are still attainable. Entrepreneurs often dream big, which is fantastic, but it's vital to ensure that your goals are grounded in reality. Assess your resources, skills, and the market environment. A goal like "I will become the leading real estate investor in my area within six months" may be too ambitious if you're just starting out. Instead, aim for smaller milestones that build towards that larger vision.

Finally, relevance and time-bound components of your goals ensure that they align with your overall business objectives and have a deadline for completion. Ask yourself how each goal furthers your mission and what timeline makes sense for achieving it. A goal such as "I will launch my new product line by the end of the year" keeps you focused and encourages consistent progress. By applying the SMART criteria, you can create a robust framework for your goals that empowers you and elevates your entrepreneurial journey.

Examples of SMART Goals for Women Entrepreneurs

Setting SMART goals is crucial for women entrepreneurs who aspire to turn their dreams into successful ventures. Each goal should be Specific, Measurable, Achievable, Relevant, and Time-bound to ensure clarity and focus. For instance, a woman entrepreneur may set a goal to increase her social media following by

25% within six months, specifying the exact metric and timeline to track progress. This type of goal not only motivates but also provides a clear pathway to achieving larger business objectives.

Another example of a SMART goal for women in real estate might involve closing five new property deals in the next quarter. This goal is Specific because it outlines the exact number of deals and Measurable since the success can be tracked through sales records. By setting a realistic and time sensitive target, the entrepreneur can develop strategies and allocate resources effectively to meet this objective.

Women freelancers can also benefit from SMART goals, such as aiming to increase their client base by 15% over the next three months. This goal is Achievable, given the freelancer's current capacity and market conditions, and Relevant to their growth aspirations. Additionally, having a deadline encourages proactive marketing efforts and enhances accountability, which is essential for maintaining momentum in a competitive landscape.

For creative entrepreneurs, a SMART goal could involve launching a new product line by the end of the year, ensuring it aligns with their brand vision. This goal is not only Specific and Time-bound but also Measurable through the number of products launched and sales generated. By mapping out a clear timeline and defining success metrics early on, these entrepreneurs can navigate the challenges of product development with confidence.

Lastly, small business owners can set SMART goals to enhance operational efficiency, such as reducing overhead costs by 10% within six months. This goal is Relevant to their financial health and Measurable through monthly expense reports. By focusing on specific strategies like renegotiating supplier contracts or optimizing workflows, women entrepreneurs can achieve meaningful improvements that contribute to long-term success.

Chapter 4: Creating Your Goal Setting Planner

Elements of an Effective Goal Setting Planner

An effective goal setting planner is a powerful tool designed to help entrepreneurs and real estate investors translate their dreams into actionable steps. It serves as a roadmap, guiding users through the complexities of setting and achieving their goals. A well structured planner not only outlines objectives but also breaks them down into manageable tasks, making it easier to navigate the entrepreneurial journey. By providing clarity and direction, a goal setting planner empowers individuals to stay focused on their aspirations and overcome challenges along the way.

One of the key elements of an effective goal setting planner is the ability to customize goals according to personal and business needs. Each entrepreneur is unique, with different visions and timelines. A planner that allows for personalization helps users to align their goals with their individual values and priorities. This customization fosters a sense of ownership and commitment, motivating them to take consistent actions toward their dreams, whether they are freelancers, solopreneurs, or small business owners.

Incorporating measurable milestones is another essential feature of a successful goal setting planner. Entrepreneurs need to track their progress to stay accountable and motivated. By establishing specific benchmarks, users can celebrate small victories along the way, which boosts morale and encourages continued effort. This quantifiable approach not only highlights progress but also allows for adjustments in strategy when necessary, ensuring that the path to success remains clear and attainable.

Moreover, an effective goal setting planner should include reflective practices that encourage users to evaluate their experiences regularly. Reflection helps entrepreneurs understand what works and what doesn't, allowing them to pivot when needed. By integrating prompts for self-assessment, a planner fosters a growth mindset, where challenges are seen as opportunities for learning and improvement. This introspective aspect is particularly valuable for women entrepreneurs, who often navigate unique hurdles in their business journeys.

Lastly, community support features can enhance the effectiveness of a goal setting planner. Networking opportunities, accountability partners, or even group challenges can inspire entrepreneurs to stay committed to their goals. A planner that encourages collaboration and connection can create a sense of belonging and shared purpose, making the pursuit of goals not just a solitary endeavor but a collective journey. This communal aspect is especially beneficial for creative entrepreneurs and those who thrive in collaborative environments.

Customizing Your Planner for Success

Customizing your planner is essential for aligning your daily actions with your long- term goals. As an entrepreneur, a real estate investor, or a freelancer, your planner should reflect your personal vision and the unique challenges of your business. Start by identifying your primary objectives and breaking them into smaller, actionable steps. This will not only make your goals feel more attainable but will also help you track your progress effectively.

Incorporate sections in your planner that cater specifically to your needs. For instance, if you're a creative entrepreneur, include brainstorming pages for ideas and inspirations. If you are a small business owner, dedicate space for client management and project timelines. By tailoring your planner, you ensure that it serves as a practical tool rather than just a decorative item.

Visual elements can enhance your planning experience. Consider using color coding to differentiate between personal and professional goals. Stickers or motivational quotes can also serve as daily reminders of your aspirations. This customization not only makes planning more enjoyable but also reinforces your commitment to achieving your objectives.

Regularly review and adjust your planner to adapt to changing circumstances. As an entrepreneur, flexibility is key to success. Set aside time each week to reflect on your accomplishments and recalibrate your goals as necessary. This dynamic approach will keep you motivated and focused, ensuring that your planner remains a relevant and powerful ally in your journey.

Lastly, remember that your planner is a reflection of you. Infuse it with your personality and values to create a space that inspires you daily. Whether it's through quotes that resonate with you or images that spark joy, your customized planner should empower you on your entrepreneurial path. Embrace the process and watch how a well tailored planner can transform the way you pursue your dreams.

Incorporating Tools and Resources

In the journey of entrepreneurship, incorporating the right tools and resources can significantly enhance your ability to achieve goals. For women entrepreneurs, utilizing goal setting planners specifically designed for their unique challenges can provide the structure and motivation needed to navigate the complexities of business ownership. These planners not only help in tracking progress but also serve as a source of inspiration, reminding you of your vision and purpose every step of the way.

Technology has made it easier than ever to access a variety of resources tailored to entrepreneurs. From digital planning apps that sync across devices to physical planners that can be personalized, the options are abundant. Finding the right combination of tools that resonate with your personal style and business needs can lead to improved productivity and focus, enabling you to turn your aspirations into actionable steps.

For real estate investors, incorporating resources such as market analysis tools and financial calculators is essential in making informed decisions. These tools can help in setting realistic financial goals and tracking the progress of investments. By integrating these resources with your goal setting planners, you can create a comprehensive strategy that aligns your business objectives with practical steps towards achieving them.

Creative entrepreneurs benefit greatly from visual tools that stimulate their imagination and help organize their ideas. Utilizing mood boards, vision boards, and creative planners can foster innovation and keep the entrepreneurial spirit alive. When you incorporate these creative resources into your overall goal setting framework, you allow yourself to explore new possibilities while remaining grounded in your goals.

Lastly, remember that your network is one of your most valuable resources. Engaging with other entrepreneurs, attending workshops, and participating in mastermind groups can provide insights and support that are instrumental in your journey. By sharing experiences and tools with like-minded individuals, you not only gain knowledge but also build a community that empowers you to reach your goals and realize your dreams as a woman entrepreneur.

Chapter 5: Short-Term vs. Long-Term Goals

Understanding the Difference

In the journey of entrepreneurship, understanding the difference between various types of goals is crucial for success. Many entrepreneurs often confuse dreams with actionable goals. While both are important, dreams represent the big picture, whereas goals are the specific steps that lead to achieving that vision. By recognizing this distinction, women entrepreneurs can create structured plans that guide them towards their aspirations.

One key aspect to consider is the difference between short-term and long-term goals. Short-term goals are actionable and can be accomplished in a relatively brief period, often serving as stepping stones towards larger, long-term objectives. For instance, a freelancer might set a short-term goal of acquiring three new clients in a month, which ultimately contributes to their long-term vision of building a sustainable business.

Emphasizing the importance of both types of goals helps in maintaining focus and motivation.

Another significant distinction lies in the difference between intrinsic and extrinsic goals. Intrinsic goals are driven by personal satisfaction and fulfillment, whereas extrinsic goals are often influenced by external rewards and recognition. For women entrepreneurs, aligning their goals with intrinsic motivations can lead to greater satisfaction and commitment to their business journey. Understanding this difference allows for more authentic goal setting that resonates with personal values and passions.

Furthermore, differentiating between individual goals and collaborative goals is vital for entrepreneurs working in teams or partnerships. Individual goals focus on personal achievement and development, while collaborative goals emphasize shared success and teamwork. By fostering a culture of collaboration and mutual support, women entrepreneurs can enhance their productivity and achieve collective milestones that benefit everyone involved.

Ultimately, understanding these differences not only enhances goal setting strategies but also empowers women entrepreneurs to navigate their unique paths with confidence. By setting clear, differentiated goals, they can track their progress, celebrate achievements, and remain resilient in the face of challenges. This clarity in goal setting paves the way for a more fulfilling entrepreneurial journey, inspiring others to follow suit.

Balancing Immediate and Future Objectives

In the journey of entrepreneurship, striking a balance between immediate and future objectives is crucial for sustained growth and success.

Entrepreneurs often find themselves caught in the whirlwind of daily tasks that demand immediate attention, such as closing deals, responding to client inquiries, and managing operational challenges. However, it is essential to remember that while these tasks are vital, they should not overshadow long-term goals that drive the overall vision of the business. Embracing a balanced approach allows entrepreneurs to navigate the day-to-day demands effectively while keeping their sights set on the bigger picture.

To achieve this balance, implementing a well-structured goal setting framework can be incredibly beneficial. Such a framework helps in categorizing objectives into immediate, short-term, and long-term goals. For instance, immediate objectives may include increasing monthly sales or enhancing customer service, while future objectives might focus on expanding into new markets or launching innovative products. By categorizing goals, entrepreneurs can allocate their time and resources more effectively, ensuring that they meet pressing demands without sacrificing their visionary pursuits.

Another critical aspect of balancing

immediate and future objectives is prioritization. Entrepreneurs should regularly assess their goals and determine which ones require immediate action and which can be scheduled for later. This prioritization process can be facilitated through tools such as goal setting planners that allow for tracking progress and making adjustments as needed. By focusing on high impact tasks that align with both immediate and long-term goals, entrepreneurs can create a more productive and fulfilling work environment.

Moreover, fostering a mindset that embraces flexibility is essential for maintaining this balance. The entrepreneurial landscape is ever evolving, and situations may arise that require a shift in focus. Being open to reassessing and recalibrating goals as circumstances change enables entrepreneurs to stay agile. This adaptability not only aids in managing current demands but also ensures that future aspirations remain attainable, even in the face of unexpected challenges.

Ultimately, finding harmony between immediate and future objectives is about creating a sustainable business model that can thrive in the long run.

Entrepreneurs who master this balance are better positioned to achieve their dreams and inspire others in their journey. By employing effective planning strategies, prioritizing wisely, and remaining flexible, women entrepreneurs can pave their way toward success, turning their visions into reality and setting a powerful example for future generations.

Strategies for Tracking Progress

Tracking progress is essential for any entrepreneur, especially for women navigating the complexities of business ownership. To effectively monitor your journey, start by establishing clear, measurable goals. This means breaking down your larger objectives into smaller, actionable steps that can be easily assessed. Regularly reviewing these goals allows you to stay aligned with your vision and adjust your strategies as needed.

Incorporating a variety of tools can enhance your tracking process. Utilize digital apps or traditional planners that cater specifically to entrepreneurs and creative individuals. These resources can help you visualize your progress through charts, checklists, or journaling. The more personalized your tracking system, the more motivated you will feel to achieve your goals.

Set specific intervals for reviewing your progress. Whether it's weekly, monthly, or quarterly, consistency is key. During these reviews, reflect on what strategies have worked and what needs adjustment. This reflection not only provides clarity but also reinforces your commitment to your goals. It's a chance to celebrate small victories, which can be incredibly empowering.

Accountability is another critical element in tracking progress. Consider finding a mentor, joining a mastermind group, or partnering with a fellow entrepreneur who shares similar goals. By being accountable to someone else, you create an additional layer of commitment to your progress. Discuss your achievements and challenges openly; this collaboration can lead to new insights and encouragement.

Finally, always remain flexible in your approach. As you track your progress, be open to altering your goals or methods if they no longer serve you. The entrepreneurial journey is rarely linear, and adaptability is a strength. Embracing change and being willing to pivot can lead to unexpected opportunities and growth, ultimately empowering you to pursue your dreams with renewed vigor.

Chapter 6: Goal Setting for Creative Entrepreneurs

Embracing Your Creativity in Goal Setting

Creativity is often perceived as a spontaneous spark of inspiration, but in goal setting, it becomes an essential tool for entrepreneurs. Embracing your creativity allows you to think outside the box, envisioning paths to success that may not be immediately apparent. When you approach your goals with a creative mindset, it not only enhances your motivation but also opens up new opportunities that align with your unique vision. This approach is vital for women entrepreneurs who are defining their own paths in competitive industries.

To effectively harness your creativity in goal setting, start by creating a vision board that reflects your aspirations. This visual representation can include images, quotes, and even symbols that resonate with your objectives. By surrounding yourself with these creative stimuli, you can keep your goals at the forefront of your mind, reminding you of the exciting possibilities that lie ahead. This practice not only fuels inspiration but also encourages you to dream bigger, fostering a deeper connection with your ambitions.

Another powerful technique is to engage in brainstorming sessions without judgment. Allow yourself the freedom to explore wild ideas, no matter how impractical they may seem. This process liberates your mind from constraints, encouraging innovative solutions to challenges you might face as an entrepreneur. Once the brainstorming is complete, you can sift through your ideas and select the most viable options to transform into actionable goals, ensuring that your creativity translates into concrete plans.

Additionally, consider integrating creative rituals into your goal setting routine. This could involve setting aside time to write in a journal, sketching your ideas, or even practicing mindfulness through meditation. Such activities not only enhance your creative flow but also help you connect with your inner self, clarifying what you truly want to achieve. By making creativity a regular part of your goal setting process, you can cultivate a mindset that embraces change and innovation, essential qualities for any entrepreneur.

Finally, remember that embracing

creativity in goal setting is not about perfection; it's about exploration and growth. Celebrate your progress, no matter how small, and be open to adjust your goals as you evolve. By fostering an environment where creativity thrives, you can empower yourself to achieve your dreams and inspire others along the way. This journey of self-discovery and creativity will not only enhance your entrepreneurial skills but also enrich your life, leading to fulfilling personal and professional experiences.

Setting Goals That Foster Innovation

Setting goals that foster innovation is essential for entrepreneurs and real estate investors who aim to stay ahead in competitive markets. Goals should not merely be a checklist to tick off but rather a dynamic framework that encourages creativity and exploration. By establishing goals that emphasize innovation, you create a pathway for new ideas and solutions to emerge, ultimately transforming challenges into opportunities for growth.

To cultivate an innovative mindset, it's crucial to set specific, measurable, attainable, relevant, and time-bound (SMART) goals.

However, in the context of innovation, these goals should also allow for flexibility and adaptation. This means incorporating milestones that encourage experimentation and learning from failures. When you embrace the possibility of change, your entrepreneurial journey can lead to uncharted territories that redefine your business potential.

Collaboration is another key element in setting goals that foster innovation. Engaging with other entrepreneurs, mentors, and even your target audience can provide fresh perspectives and insights. By integrating diverse viewpoints into your goal setting process, you not only expand your horizons but also create a culture of inclusivity that can drive innovative solutions. Building a network of like-minded individuals encourages brainstorming sessions and shared accountability, which are vital for sustained innovation.

Regularly reviewing and adjusting your goals is also essential in maintaining an innovative edge. The business landscape is constantly evolving, and your goals should reflect these changes. Establish a routine for assessing your progress and the relevance of your objectives. This ongoing evaluation process allows you to pivot when necessary and ensures that your goals continue to inspire and challenge you, keeping the spirit of innovation alive.

Ultimately, setting goals that foster innovation is about creating a vision that is both aspirational and achievable. By embracing creativity, collaboration, and flexibility, you can transform your entrepreneurial journey into one that not only meets your dreams but also inspires those around you. Remember, the most successful entrepreneurs are those who dare to dream big and take bold steps towards realizing those dreams, making innovation a fundamental part of their growth strategy.

Case Studies of Successful Creative Entrepreneurs

In the ever evolving landscape of entrepreneurship, case studies of successful creative entrepreneurs serve as powerful testaments to the potential of innovative thinking and strategic goal setting. One such example is Sara Blakely, the founder of Spanx. Starting with just $5,000, she combined her vision with a relentless determination to create a revolutionary product in women's undergarments. Her journey illustrates how setting clear goals and maintaining focus can lead to remarkable success, inspiring countless women and aspiring entrepreneurs to pursue their dreams with tenacity.

Another inspiring case is that of Lisa Congdon, an artist and entrepreneur who transformed her passion for art into a thriving business. After starting her career later in life, Congdon utilized effective goal setting techniques to build her brand, leading to collaborations with major companies and a robust online presence. Her story highlights the importance of adaptability and the courage to step outside one's comfort zone, proving that it's never too late to achieve ambitious goals.

The journey of Rachel Hollis, a best-selling author and motivational speaker, also exemplifies the power of strategic planning. Hollis began her career as a wedding planner but shifted her focus to share her personal development insights with a broader audience. By establishing clear objectives and leveraging social media, she grew her brand significantly. Her case underscores the importance of identifying one's unique voice and utilizing it to connect with others, a valuable lesson for aspiring entrepreneurs in any niche.

Additionally, consider the story of Jenna

Kutcher, a photographer and online educator who began her career while working a full-time job. Kutcher effectively used goal setting to transition from part-time to full-time entrepreneurship, ultimately building a successful brand that empowers others. Her ability to set realistic milestones and celebrate small wins along the way is a testament to the impact of incremental progress, inspiring freelancers and solopreneurs to take actionable steps toward their dreams.

These case studies illuminate the diverse paths that creative entrepreneurs can take to achieve their goals. Each story emphasizes the importance of resilience, adaptability, and the power of a well-structured plan. By learning from these successful women, aspiring entrepreneurs can cultivate their unique strategies and pursue their dreams with confidence and clarity, knowing that the journey is as important as the destination.

Chapter 7: Goal Setting for Freelancers and Solopreneurs

Unique Challenges and Opportunities

The journey of a woman entrepreneur is often fraught with unique challenges that can feel overwhelming. Balancing professional ambitions with personal responsibilities can create a juggling act that demands resilience and creativity. Women often face societal expectations that can hinder their pursuit of entrepreneurial goals, yet these challenges can also serve as catalysts for innovation and determination. By recognizing these hurdles, women can devise strategies that not only help them overcome obstacles but also empower them to carve their own paths in the business world.

In the realm of real estate investment, women entrepreneurs may encounter barriers such as limited access to funding and mentorship. These hurdles can initially seem daunting, but they present opportunities to build supportive networks and seek alternative financing options. By collaborating with other women in the industry, entrepreneurs can share resources and insights that enhance their chances of success. Embracing these opportunities can lead to a more inclusive and diverse real estate market, ultimately benefiting all investors involved.

Goal setting is an essential tool for any entrepreneur, but women often need to tailor their approaches to suit their unique circumstances. Customizable goal setting planners can serve as invaluable resources, allowing women to align their business objectives with personal values and aspirations. These planners can help women visualize their goals, break them down into manageable steps, and track their progress, fostering a sense of accountability and accomplishment. By using these tools, women can transform their dreams into actionable plans that resonate with their individual journeys.

Moreover, the rise of the digital age has opened new avenues for women entrepreneurs to explore. Online platforms provide access to global markets, enabling them to reach wider audiences and expand their businesses beyond local borders. This opportunity encourages women to think creatively about their offerings and marketing strategies, allowing them to leverage their unique perspectives. By embracing technology and digital tools, women can enhance their visibility and create impactful brands that reflect their values and missions.

Ultimately, the unique challenges faced by women entrepreneurs can lead to profound growth and success. By reframing obstacles as opportunities, women can cultivate resilience and foster innovation in their ventures. The path may be filled with twists and turns, but with the right mindset and resources, women entrepreneurs can not only achieve their goals but also inspire future generations of women to pursue their dreams fearlessly. The journey is as significant as the destination, and every step taken is a testament to their strength and determination.

Building a Flexible Goal Framework

Building a flexible goal framework is an essential step for entrepreneurs and real estate investors who want to achieve their dreams without feeling constrained by rigid plans. This framework allows for adaptability, ensuring that as circumstances and priorities change, your goals can evolve accordingly. Embracing flexibility not only fosters creativity but also empowers you to take advantage of new opportunities that arise in your entrepreneurial journey.

To create this flexible framework, start by identifying your core values and long-term vision. Understanding what truly matters to you will serve as the foundation for your goals. Once you have a clear vision, break it down into smaller, actionable steps that can be adjusted as needed. Each step should be realistic and achievable, allowing for a sense of progress while maintaining the freedom to pivot when necessary.

Incorporating regular reviews into your goal setting process is crucial for maintaining flexibility. Schedule time to assess your progress, reflect on what's working, and identify areas that may need adjustment. This practice not only keeps you accountable but also encourages a mindset of continuous improvement. Remember, your goals should serve you, not the other way around.

Collaboration and networking with other entrepreneurs can also enhance your flexible goal framework. Sharing experiences, challenges, and successes with peers can provide new insights and perspectives that help you refine your goals. Participate in mastermind groups or seek mentorship to gain valuable feedback and encouragement, which can inspire you to think outside the box and approach your goals with renewed energy.

Finally, don't be afraid to celebrate your achievements, no matter how small. Each milestone reached is a testament to your hard work and dedication. Acknowledging these wins not only boosts your motivation but also reinforces the importance of flexibility in your journey. By building a flexible goal framework, you empower yourself to navigate the ever changing landscape of entrepreneurship with confidence and resilience.

Time Management and Productivity Tips

Time management is a crucial skill for any entrepreneur, especially for women navigating the challenges of business. By implementing effective strategies, you can enhance your productivity and focus on what truly matters. Start by prioritizing your tasks using the Eisenhower Matrix, which allows you to categorize tasks based on urgency and importance. This approach helps in identifying which tasks deserve your immediate attention and which can be delegated or postponed, enabling you to make the most of your time.

Another effective method is to establish a daily routine that aligns with your peak productivity hours. Understanding when you are most alert and focused can significantly influence your work output. For many, early mornings may provide the quiet and calm needed to tackle complex tasks, while others may thrive in the afternoon. Incorporating dedicated time blocks for specific tasks and breaks can help maintain your energy levels throughout the day.

Setting clear, achievable goals is essential for maintaining productivity. Using guided goal setting planners can help you define your objectives and break them down into manageable steps. This not only keeps you on track but also allows for regular reflection on your progress. Celebrate small wins along the way to maintain motivation and reinforce your commitment to your larger goals.

Eliminating distractions is another critical element of effective time management. Create a workspace that minimizes interruptions, whether by setting boundaries with family during work hours or utilizing apps that limit social media usage.

Additionally, consider scheduling regular check-ins with yourself to assess your focus and productivity levels, making adjustments as necessary to stay aligned with your goals.

Lastly, remember that self-care plays a vital role in productivity. Taking time for yourself to recharge can enhance your creativity and problem solving abilities. Prioritize activities that nourish your mind and body, such as exercise, meditation, or simply enjoying time with loved ones. By balancing work with self-care, you foster a sustainable approach to achieving your entrepreneurial dreams.

Chapter 8: The Role of Accountability

Finding Accountability Partners

Finding accountability partners can be a transformative step in your entrepreneurial journey. These partners can provide the motivation and support necessary to keep you focused on your goals. As a woman entrepreneur, connecting with others who understand your challenges can foster a sense of community and encouragement that is invaluable. By sharing your aspirations and challenges with someone else, you create a powerful alliance that can amplify your success.

Start by identifying individuals within your network who share similar ambitions. This could be fellow entrepreneurs, mentors, or even friends who are also pursuing their professional dreams. Look for people who inspire you, challenge you, and are committed to their own growth. Establishing a mutual relationship where each party feels accountable to the other is essential. This synergy can help both of you stay on track and push each other toward achieving your goals.

Consider joining entrepreneurial groups or networking events tailored for women. These spaces can provide a fertile ground for finding potential accountability partners. Not only will you meet like-minded individuals, but you'll also benefit from shared experiences and insights that can enhance your goal setting process. Engaging with a community of women who are navigating similar paths can foster lasting relationships that support your entrepreneurial journey.

Once you've found a potential partner, set clear expectations for your accountability relationship. Discuss how often you will check in with each other, the methods of communication you prefer, and the specific goals you want to hold each other accountable for. Whether it's weekly meetings or monthly progress reports, having a structured approach can increase the effectiveness of your partnership. Accountability thrives on consistency, so make sure you both prioritize your meetings.

Lastly, celebrate each other's achievements, no matter how small. Acknowledging progress fosters a positive environment and encourages both partners to continue pushing forward. As you share your successes and setbacks, you'll build a deeper connection that enhances both your personal and professional growth. Finding accountability partners is not just about achieving goals; it's about creating a supportive network that empowers you to dream bigger and achieve more.

The Power of Mentorship

Mentorship is a cornerstone of success in the entrepreneurial journey, particularly for women striving to carve their niche in competitive fields like real estate and creative industries. Having a mentor can provide invaluable insights, guidance, and encouragement, helping entrepreneurs navigate the complexities of their ventures. A mentor not only shares their experiences but also opens doors to networks that can be crucial for growth and opportunity.

In the realm of goal setting, mentors can play a transformative role. They help clarify objectives, break down overwhelming tasks into manageable steps, and instill the confidence needed to pursue ambitious dreams. Whether it's setting targets for a new business initiative or refining a creative project, a mentor's perspective can illuminate pathways that might not be immediately visible. This guidance is especially vital for freelancers and solopreneurs who often work in isolation.

Mentorship also fosters accountability, a critical factor in achieving goals. With a mentor's support, entrepreneurs are more likely to stay focused on their objectives, regularly checking in on progress and adjusting strategies as necessary. This relationship encourages a proactive approach, ensuring that women entrepreneurs are not just dreaming but also taking actionable steps toward their aspirations.

Additionally, the emotional support provided by a mentor can be a game changer. Entrepreneurship is fraught with challenges, and having someone who understands the unique struggles faced by women in business can make a significant difference. This supportive relationship can cultivate resilience and inspire an unwavering belief in one's capabilities, which is essential for overcoming obstacles and achieving long-term success.

Ultimately, the power of mentorship lies in its ability to inspire growth and foster connections. By seeking out mentors, women entrepreneurs can not only enhance their skills and knowledge but also create a community that uplifts and empowers. This collaborative spirit is what transforms individual ambitions into collective achievements, propelling women to realize their dreams and set new standards in entrepreneurship.

Creating Accountability Systems

Creating accountability systems is essential for any entrepreneur looking to turn their dreams into reality. These systems act as frameworks that help you stay on track with your goals, providing structure and support in your journey. Whether you are a real estate investor, a creative entrepreneur, or a solopreneur, establishing an accountability system can help you focus on your priorities and enhance your productivity.

One effective method of creating accountability is through partnerships or accountability groups. Collaborating with like-minded individuals fosters a sense of community and shared responsibility. You can set regular meetings to discuss progress, share challenges, and celebrate successes. This mutual encouragement not only keeps you accountable but also enhances your motivation to achieve your goals.

Another strategy is to utilize goal setting planners tailored to your specific needs. These planners can help you break down larger objectives into manageable tasks, making it easier to monitor your progress. By customizing your planner to fit your unique entrepreneurial journey, you can create a personalized roadmap that aligns with your aspirations, ensuring that you remain focused and accountable for your actions.

Incorporating technology can also play a vital role in maintaining accountability. Various apps and tools are available that allow you to track your goals, set reminders, and connect with peers for support. Leveraging these resources can help streamline your accountability processes, making it easier to stay organized and committed to your objectives.

Lastly, reflecting on your progress regularly is crucial in any accountability system. Set aside time each week or month to review what you've accomplished and where you need to improve. This reflection not only helps you recognize your achievements but also reinforces your commitment to your goals, ensuring that you remain on the path to success. By integrating these practices into your routine, you will cultivate a robust accountability system that empowers you to achieve your dreams.

Chapter 9:
Celebrating
Milestones

Recognizing and
Rewarding Progress

Recognizing and rewarding progress is
essential for maintaining motivation and
momentum in any entrepreneurial
journey. As women entrepreneurs, it is
vital to celebrate even the smallest
victories along the way.

Each milestone achieved, whether it's
closing a deal, launching a new product,
or simply sticking to a daily routine,

deserves acknowledgment. This practice not only uplifts your spirit but also reinforces a positive mindset that fuels further achievements.

One effective way to recognize progress is through journaling. Keeping a dedicated journal where you document your goals and reflect on your accomplishments can provide valuable insights into your growth. Reviewing past entries allows you to see how far you've come, which can be incredibly empowering. Moreover, sharing your journey with fellow entrepreneurs or a mentor can enhance this experience, as they can offer encouragement and celebrate your achievements alongside you.

Rewards can take many forms, and it is important to personalize them to fit your preferences. Whether it's treating yourself to a spa day, a nice dinner, or investing in a new tool for your business, find what makes you feel appreciated. Setting up a reward system linked to specific milestones can also create a sense of accountability and excitement. These rewards serve as tangible reminders of your hard work and dedication, reinforcing your commitment to your goals.

Additionally, fostering a culture of recognition within your network is beneficial. Encourage peers and colleagues to celebrate each other's successes, creating an environment where progress is valued. This mutual support can lead to stronger relationships and a more collaborative atmosphere, which is essential for growth. When everyone actively recognizes achievements, it builds a community that thrives on positivity and encouragement, further motivating each individual to reach their goals.

Finally, don't forget to recognize your own journey by practicing self-compassion. As you navigate the ups and downs of entrepreneurship, be kind to yourself.

Understand that setbacks are part of the process, and they do not diminish your achievements. Embrace the journey, celebrate progress, and keep moving forward with confidence. By recognizing and rewarding your progress, you empower not only yourself but also inspire those around you to pursue their dreams with vigor.

Reflecting on Achievements

Reflecting on achievements is a powerful

practice that can elevate your mindset and propel you toward future success. As entrepreneurs, it's easy to get caught up in the hustle and bustle of daily tasks and long-term goals. However, taking a moment to recognize what you have accomplished can serve as a motivational boost, reminding you of your capabilities and the progress you've made. This reflection not only reinforces your confidence but also helps in recalibrating your strategies for the future.

When you pause to celebrate your milestones, big or small, you acknowledge the hard work and dedication that went into reaching those points. This acknowledgment can help you appreciate the journey, including the challenges and setbacks you've faced along the way. Each achievement is a testament to your resilience and creativity as a business owner, and recognizing them can ignite a renewed sense of purpose and passion for your work.

Consider keeping a dedicated journal for reflecting on your achievements. Such a journal can serve as a tangible reminder of your journey and progress. Each entry can detail not just the successes, but also the lessons learned, the skills developed, and the connections made throughout the process.

This practice can be especially beneficial for women entrepreneurs, who often juggle multiple roles and responsibilities, providing a moment of clarity and pride in their unique paths.

Moreover, sharing your achievements with others can foster community and support among fellow entrepreneurs. By discussing your successes, you can inspire others to reflect on their own journeys, creating a positive feedback loop that fuels motivation. Networking events, social media, or even casual meet-ups can become platforms for sharing stories of triumph, reinforcing the idea that we are all part of a larger ecosystem of support and encouragement.

In conclusion, reflecting on your achievements is not just about self-recognition; it's a critical practice that can enhance your entrepreneurial journey. It allows you to celebrate your progress, learn from your experiences, and connect with others. As you continue to set and pursue your goals, remember that taking the time to reflect is essential in maintaining momentum and cultivating a success-driven mindset.

Setting New Goals After Success

Success is a powerful catalyst that can drive entrepreneurs to reevaluate their aspirations and set new goals. After achieving a milestone, it's essential to take a moment to reflect on what contributed to that success. This reflection not only reinforces the positive actions taken but also illuminates areas for potential growth. By understanding the journey that led to success, entrepreneurs can gain clarity on their next steps, ensuring that their future goals are both ambitious and achievable.

Once reflection is complete, it's time to

dream big again. Setting new goals
should be a blend of personal ambition
and market opportunities.

Entrepreneurs, especially women, are
encouraged to think outside the box and
pursue goals that resonate with their
passions and values. This could mean
expanding existing businesses, exploring
new markets, or even venturing into
completely different fields. Embracing
creativity in goal-setting allows for
innovative solutions that can lead to
unexpected successes.

Additionally, the importance of
community support cannot be
overstated. Surrounding oneself with

like-minded individuals who share similar aspirations can provide motivation and inspiration. Networking with fellow entrepreneurs and real estate investors can also lead to collaborative opportunities that enhance business growth. These relationships often offer invaluable advice and encouragement, making the journey toward new goals feel less daunting and more achievable.

As you set new goals, consider integrating a structured approach to your planning. Utilizing goal setting planners tailored for entrepreneurs can help streamline the process, making it easier to visualize objectives and track progress.

Such planners often include resources for breaking down larger goals into actionable steps, setting deadlines, and maintaining accountability. For women entrepreneurs, having a guided approach can be especially empowering, ensuring that goals are not only set but also pursued with determination and clarity.

Finally, remember that the journey of entrepreneurship is an ongoing process of learning and adaptation. Setting new goals after success is not just about aiming higher but also about evolving as a business leader. Embrace the challenges that come with new aspirations, and celebrate the small victories along the way. Each goal achieved builds momentum and confidence, paving the way for even greater accomplishments in the future.

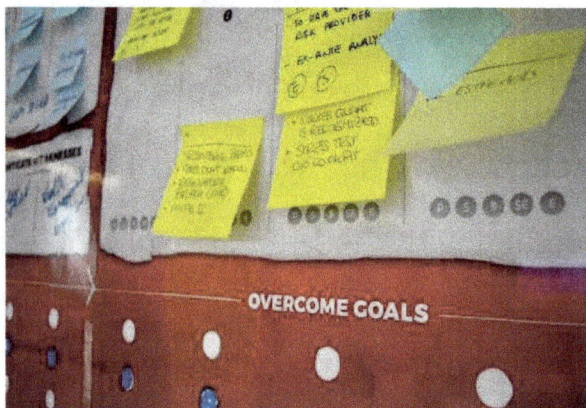

Chapter 10: Staying Motivated through Challenges

Cultivating Resilience

Resilience is a crucial trait for entrepreneurs, especially women navigating the complexities of business ownership. Cultivating resilience involves developing the mental fortitude to bounce back from setbacks and persist in the face of challenges. For women entrepreneurs, this means embracing failures as learning opportunities and not as definitive endpoints. By fostering a growth mindset, you can view each obstacle as a stepping stone toward your ultimate goals, making resilience an essential part of your journey.

One effective method of cultivating resilience is through the practice of self-reflection. Regularly taking the time to assess your experiences—both good and bad—can provide valuable insights into your strengths and areas for improvement. Journaling can be an excellent tool for this purpose, allowing you to track your progress, set new goals, and celebrate small victories along the way. By recognizing your achievements, no matter how minor, you build a reservoir of confidence that fuels your resilience.

Another important aspect of resilience is building a supportive network. Surrounding yourself with like-minded individuals can provide encouragement and motivation during tough times.

Whether through local networking events, online communities, or mentorship programs, connecting with other women entrepreneurs creates a sense of camaraderie. Sharing experiences and strategies not only helps you navigate challenges but also reinforces the idea that you are not alone in your journey.

Setting realistic goals is also essential for developing resilience. Break your larger aspirations into manageable milestones and celebrate each achievement. This approach not only keeps you focused but also allows you to recognize your progress, fostering a sense of accomplishment. When you experience setbacks, having a clear roadmap helps you regain your footing more quickly, as you can re-evaluate your strategy without losing sight of your end goals.

Finally, remember that resilience is a skill that can be developed over time. It requires patience and practice, just like any other entrepreneurial skill. By consistently applying these techniques in your daily life, you'll find yourself not only achieving your goals but also becoming more adaptable and innovative in your approach. Embrace the journey of cultivating resilience, and watch as it transforms your entrepreneurial experience into one filled with growth, success, and fulfillment.

Overcoming Setbacks

Setbacks are an inevitable part of any entrepreneurial journey. They can manifest as financial losses, failed projects, or even personal challenges that threaten to derail your progress.

Instead of viewing these obstacles as insurmountable, it's essential to adopt a mindset that sees them as valuable learning experiences. Embracing setbacks allows you to assess what went wrong and develop strategies to prevent similar issues in the future. One key strategy for overcoming setbacks is to maintain a strong support network.

Surrounding yourself with like-minded individuals who understand the entrepreneurial journey can provide the encouragement you need during tough times. These connections can offer diverse perspectives and insights that may help you reframe your challenges and see them as stepping stones rather than roadblocks. Engaging in networking events or joining entrepreneurial groups can significantly enhance your resilience.

Another critical aspect of overcoming setbacks is the practice of self-reflection. Taking the time to analyze your experiences can lead to profound personal and professional growth. Journaling about your challenges, feelings, and lessons learned can clarify your thoughts and reinforce your commitment to your goals. This reflection phase is not just about identifying what went wrong but also recognizing your strengths and the progress you've made despite difficulties.

Setting realistic and flexible goals can also help you navigate setbacks more effectively. When you understand that the path to success is not linear, you can adjust your expectations and remain focused on your long-term vision. Using goal setting planners can aid in creating a roadmap that accommodates both your ambitions and the inevitable twists and turns of your journey.

This adaptability will empower you to keep moving forward, even when faced with adversity.

Finally, remember that resilience is built over time. Each setback you encounter is an opportunity to strengthen your resolve and enhance your skills.

Celebrate small victories along the way, as they can provide motivation during challenging periods. By cultivating a resilient mindset, you can transform setbacks into powerful catalysts for growth, ensuring that every challenge propels you closer to your entrepreneurial dreams.

Maintaining Momentum

Maintaining momentum is crucial for any entrepreneur, especially for women steering their own ships in the dynamic waters of business. As the excitement of launching a new project or venture begins to fade, it's essential to find ways to keep that initial enthusiasm alive. This involves regularly revisiting your goals, celebrating small wins, and keeping your vision clear. By doing so, you not only reinforce your commitment to your ambitions but also create a sustainable path forward.

One effective strategy for maintaining momentum is to establish a routine that includes consistent goal setting. This can be as simple as setting aside time each week to reflect on your progress and adjust your plans as necessary. Utilizing goal setting planners tailored for entrepreneurs can provide structure and clarity. These planners can help you map out your objectives, prioritize tasks, and maintain focus, ensuring that each step you take aligns with your long-term vision.

Another vital aspect of sustaining momentum is surrounding yourself with a supportive network. Engaging with fellow entrepreneurs, whether through networking events or online communities, can provide motivation and inspiration. Sharing experiences, challenges, and victories not only fosters accountability but also opens doors to new ideas and collaborations. The energy generated by like-minded individuals can be incredibly contagious and can help you push through obstacles.

Additionally, don't underestimate the power of self-care in maintaining your momentum. As entrepreneurs, it's easy to get caught up in the hustle and forget to recharge. Taking breaks to nurture your mental and physical health is essential for long-term success. Incorporating mindfulness practices, exercise, or simply taking time off can rejuvenate your spirit and spark creativity, allowing you to return to your goals with renewed energy and focus.

Finally, remember that maintaining momentum is a journey, not a destination. It requires constant adjustment and a willingness to evolve as circumstances change. Embrace setbacks as learning opportunities and stay adaptable. By cultivating resilience and optimism, you can keep the fire of your entrepreneurial spirit burning bright, ensuring that you not only achieve your dreams but also enjoy the journey along the way.

Chapter 11: The Future of Your Goals

Reevaluating and Adjusting Goals

As women entrepreneurs, we often set ambitious goals that reflect our dreams and aspirations. However, the journey of entrepreneurship is rarely linear, and it is crucial to reassess our goals periodically. Reevaluating our objectives allows us to adapt to changing circumstances, whether they arise from market fluctuations, personal growth, or shifts in our business environment. By taking the time to reflect on our goals, we can ensure they remain aligned with our core values and long-term vision.

Adjusting our goals does not signify failure; rather, it is a mark of growth and resilience. Entrepreneurs must embrace the idea that flexibility is a strength. When we encounter obstacles or realize that our ambitions have evolved, it is essential to modify our goals accordingly. This practice not only enhances our focus but also cultivates a growth mindset that empowers us to overcome challenges and seize new opportunities.

To effectively reevaluate and adjust our goals, we should engage in regular self-assessment. This can involve setting aside time each month or quarter to review our progress and reflect on what has worked and what hasn't. Utilizing goal setting planners tailored for entrepreneurs can be instrumental in this process. These tools provide a structured framework to document our goals, track milestones, and analyze results, making it easier to identify areas that require adjustment.

Additionally, seeking feedback from mentors, peers, or even clients can offer valuable insights into our goal setting strategies. Their perspectives may reveal blind spots we hadn't considered and inspire us to think differently about our objectives. Remember, collaboration and learning from others are essential components of the entrepreneurial journey, and they can significantly influence our ability to adapt and thrive.

In conclusion, reevaluating and adjusting our goals is a continual process that reflects our commitment to personal and professional growth. By maintaining flexibility, engaging in self-assessment, and seeking external feedback, we can ensure our goals remain relevant and inspiring. This approach not only drives us toward our dreams but also empowers us to navigate the ever evolving landscape of entrepreneurship with confidence and clarity.

Embracing Lifelong Learning

In today's fast-paced world, embracing lifelong learning is not just an option; it's a necessity for entrepreneurs and real estate investors. The landscape of business is constantly evolving, and staying ahead requires a commitment to continuous education and skill enhancement. By cultivating a mindset geared towards learning, you empower yourself to adapt to changes, seize opportunities, and ultimately achieve your goals. This mindset is particularly crucial for women entrepreneurs who often juggle multiple roles and responsibilities, making effective time management and learning strategies essential.

One effective approach to lifelong learning is setting specific, actionable goals. Goal setting planners designed for entrepreneurs can be instrumental in this process. They provide a structured way to identify what skills or knowledge you want to acquire and set timelines for achieving these objectives. By using these planners, you can break down your learning journey into manageable steps, making it easier to track your progress and stay motivated. This method not only enhances your capabilities but also boosts your confidence as you see tangible results from your efforts.

Networking plays a critical role in lifelong learning as well. Engaging with other entrepreneurs, attending workshops, and participating in industry events can expose you to new ideas and perspectives. These interactions can inspire innovative solutions to challenges you may face in your business.

Additionally, surrounding yourself with like-minded individuals fosters a supportive environment that encourages growth and collaboration. Remember, learning from others' experiences can save you time and resources while providing invaluable insights.

Incorporating technology into your lifelong learning strategy can significantly enhance your knowledge acquisition. Online courses, webinars, and podcasts offer flexibility and access to a wealth of information that fits into your busy schedule. As a woman entrepreneur, leveraging these resources allows you to learn at your own pace and focus on areas that align with your business goals. By diversifying your learning methods, you can ensure that you remain engaged and inspired throughout your journey.

Lastly, it's essential to reflect on your learning experiences regularly. Taking the time to evaluate what you've learned and how it applies to your business helps solidify your new knowledge. This reflection can lead to deeper insights and assist you in adjusting your goals and strategies as needed.

Remember, the journey of lifelong learning is ongoing, and by embracing it, you not only empower yourself but also set an inspiring example for other women entrepreneurs who aspire to achieve their dreams.

Inspiring Others with Your Journey

Every entrepreneur's journey is unique and filled with challenges that can inspire others. By sharing your experiences, whether they are triumphs or setbacks, you create a relatable narrative that resonates with fellow entrepreneurs. This act of vulnerability not only empowers you but also encourages those around you to embrace their own journeys with courage and determination. Remember, your story can be the spark that ignites someone else's dream.

Inspiring others begins with authenticity. When you share your genuine experiences, it fosters a connection that transcends the typical mentor-mentee relationship. People are drawn to real stories that reflect the complexities of entrepreneurship. By showcasing your challenges and how you overcame them, you provide valuable insights that others can learn from, making your journey a roadmap for aspiring entrepreneurs.

Moreover, storytelling can be a powerful tool for goal setting. As you outline your path, highlight the specific goals you set and the strategies you implemented to achieve them. This not only provides a framework for others to follow but also illustrates the importance of setting clear, actionable goals. By demonstrating how goal setting played a pivotal role in your success, you inspire others to adopt similar practices in their own ventures.

Creating a community of support is another vital aspect of inspiring others. When you share your journey, you invite others to do the same, fostering an environment where experiences are exchanged, and advice is given. This sense of community can be particularly empowering for women entrepreneurs who often face unique challenges in the business world. By uplifting each other, you not only inspire but also create a network that encourages persistence and resilience.

Finally, remember that inspiration is a cycle. As you uplift others with your journey, you, in turn, are inspired by their stories. This reciprocal relationship fuels creativity and innovation within the entrepreneurial community. Your journey is not just yours; it belongs to everyone who finds motivation in your experiences. Embrace this ripple effect, and continue to share your story, for it has the power to change lives and empower future generations of entrepreneurs.

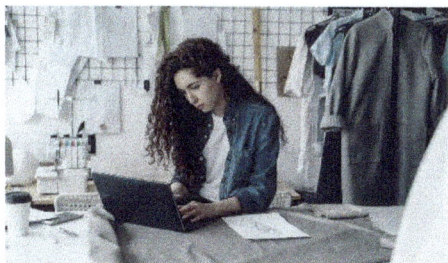

Chapter 12:
Resources and Tools
for Women
Entrepreneurs

Recommended Books and
Podcasts

In the journey of entrepreneurship, knowledge is power. To empower yourself in achieving your goals, delving into insightful books can provide the guidance and inspiration needed to navigate the challenges of running a business. Books such as "Girl, Stop

Apologizing" by Rachel Hollis and "The Lean Startup" by Eric Ries offer valuable perspectives on goal setting, productivity, and resilience. These authors share their experiences and practical advice, helping women entrepreneurs and creative freelancers alike to foster a mindset of growth and determination.

Podcasts are another excellent resource for entrepreneurs looking to gain insights on goal achievement. Shows like "How I Built This" with Guy Raz and "The Goal Digger Podcast" by Jenna Kutcher feature interviews with successful entrepreneurs who share their stories, struggles, and strategies. Listening to these stories can spark motivation and provide real world applications of goal setting principles, making it easier for solopreneurs and small business owners to implement them in their journeys.

When choosing books and podcasts, consider those that resonate with your personal experiences and aspirations. For instance, "Big Magic" by Elizabeth Gilbert encourages creative entrepreneurs to embrace their curiosity and pursue their passions fearlessly. Similarly, "The Mindset Mentor" podcast provides actionable advice on cultivating a positive mindset, which is crucial for overcoming obstacles and achieving your goals.

Creating a list of recommended reads and listens can serve as a resource for your entrepreneurial community. Sharing these recommendations not only helps others but also reinforces your own learning. As you discuss the insights gained from these materials, you can foster discussions that lead to further growth and inspiration among peers in real estate investing and beyond.

Lastly, remember that the journey of entrepreneurship is not a solitary one. Engaging with a community of like-minded individuals through book clubs or podcast listening groups can enhance your learning experience. Together, you can celebrate successes, share challenges, and set collective goals, creating an environment that empowers all to reach their dreams.

Goal Setting Apps and Software

In today's fast-paced world, goal setting apps and software have become essential tools for women entrepreneurs striving to achieve

their dreams. These digital solutions empower users to establish clear objectives, track progress, and stay motivated throughout their journeys. With various features tailored to the unique needs of entrepreneurs, real estate investors, and freelancers, these applications provide a structured approach to goal achievement, enabling users to focus on their aspirations without becoming overwhelmed.

One of the significant advantages of goal setting apps is their accessibility. Entrepreneurs can easily download and access these tools on their smartphones or tablets, making it convenient to set and update goals on the go. Many of these platforms offer customizable templates that cater specifically to women entrepreneurs and small business owners, ensuring that users can create a personalized goal setting experience that aligns with their unique aspirations and challenges.

Furthermore, goal setting software often includes features such as reminders, progress tracking, and analytics. These functionalities allow users to visualize their achievements, which can be incredibly motivating. By breaking larger goals into manageable tasks, entrepreneurs can maintain momentum and celebrate small victories along the way. This process not only enhances productivity but also fosters a sense of accomplishment and confidence in their abilities.

Collaboration is another key benefit of many goal setting applications. Entrepreneurs working in teams can share goals, assign tasks, and provide feedback in real-time. This collaborative environment encourages accountability and support among team members, making it easier to stay aligned and motivated towards common objectives. For creative entrepreneurs and freelancers, this aspect is particularly beneficial, as it allows for the integration of diverse ideas and perspectives into the goal setting process.

In conclusion, embracing goal setting apps and software is a powerful step for women entrepreneurs ready to take charge of their futures. By leveraging these tools, they can create a structured yet flexible framework for achieving their dreams. Whether you're a solo entrepreneur or part of a larger team, the right goal setting application can empower you to turn your visions into reality and propel your business forward with clarity and purpose.

Building a Supportive Community

Building a supportive community is

essential for women entrepreneurs striving to achieve their goals. This community serves as a foundation where ideas can flourish, experiences can be shared, and encouragement is abundant. By surrounding yourself with like-minded individuals, you create an environment that fosters growth, collaboration, and mutual support. Whether you are a freelancer, a small business owner, or an investor, having a network that understands your journey can make all the difference in your entrepreneurial success.

One of the first steps in building a supportive community is to seek out networking opportunities. Attend industry conferences, join local business groups, or participate in online forums tailored to your niche. These spaces are not just for making connections; they are platforms where you can learn from others, share your challenges, and celebrate your victories. Engaging with fellow entrepreneurs can provide you with fresh perspectives and innovative ideas that can propel your business forward.

Furthermore, consider forming or joining mastermind groups. These small, focused gatherings allow you to dive deeper into specific goals while receiving constructive feedback from peers. In a mastermind group, members hold each other accountable, which is crucial in maintaining momentum towards achieving your objectives. The collective wisdom and varied experiences of group members can inspire new strategies and solutions that you may not have thought of on your own.

It's also important to cultivate a spirit of giving within your community. Offer your support, whether it's through mentoring, sharing resources, or celebrating others' achievements. When you contribute to the success of your peers, you create a culture of reciprocity that enriches everyone involved.

This not only strengthens your relationships but also establishes a sense of belonging, which is vital for personal and professional growth.

Lastly, remember that building a supportive community takes time and effort. Be patient and persistent in nurturing these connections. Celebrate the small wins along the way, and don't hesitate to reach out when you need help. Every entrepreneur faces obstacles, but with a strong community behind you, those challenges become much easier to navigate.

Together, you can lift each other higher and achieve the dreams you've set out to accomplish.